D1075288

PS
3565
C5.7
27

UNIVERSITY OF MINNESOTA

⤴ *Flannery O'Connor*

DISCARDED

BY STANLEY EDGAR HYMAN

NORMANDALE STATE JUNIOR COLLEGE
9700 FRANCE AVENUE SOUTH
BLOOMINGTON, MINNESOTA 55431

UNIVERSITY OF MINNESOTA PRESS · MINNEAPOLIS

© Copyright 1966 by the University of Minnesota

ALL RIGHTS RESERVED

Printed in the United States of America at
the North Central Publishing Company, St. Paul

Library of Congress Catalog Card Number: 66-63486

The author wishes to thank Bennington College for a sabbatical leave; the Huber Foundation for a grant enabling him to do research in Milledgeville, Ga.; Regina O'Connor and her neighbors for many kindnesses; Robert Fitzgerald for permission to quote from unpublished materials; the *New Leader* for permission to reprint material it first published; all who helped supply material, especially Frederick J. Asals, Jr., and Granville Hicks; and colleagues who read the manuscript, along with Catharine Carver and Barbara Karmiller. The author's indebtedness to Joseph Mitchell is inadequately acknowledged in the dedication; his indebtedness to the late Shirley Jackson is beyond the possibility of acknowledgment.

Distributed to high schools in the United States by Webster Division
McGraw-Hill Book Company
St. Louis   New York   San Francisco   Dallas

PUBLISHED IN GREAT BRITAIN, INDIA, AND PAKISTAN BY THE OXFORD
UNIVERSITY PRESS, LONDON, BOMBAY, AND KARACHI, AND IN CANADA
BY THE COPP CLARK PUBLISHING CO. LIMITED, TORONTO

TO JOSEPH MITCHELL

STANLY EDGAR HYMAN, who teaches at Bennington Colleɜ, is a staff writer for the *New Yorker* and author or edor of numerous books, the latest being *The Promed End*. He has also written another pamphlet in this series, *Nathanael West*.

⤳ *Flannery O'Connor*

M ARY FLANNERY O'CONNOR was born in Savannah, Georgia, on March 25, 1925. She was the only child of Regina L. Cline and Edward F. O'Connor, Jr. Both families were Roman Catholic. The Clines were a prominent family in the state, Regina Cline's father having been mayor of Milledgeville for many years.

Mary Flannery grew up as rather a solitary child until she attended parochial school. She loved pet fowl all her life. When she was five, an aunt gave her, as a curiosity, a bantam chicken that walked backwards, and it was this that led to her first national celebrity. The Pathé News people filmed little Mary O'Connor with her trained chicken, and showed the film around the country.

In 1938 Edward O'Connor was discovered to have disseminated lupus, an incurable disease in which the body forms antibodies to its own tissues. The O'Connors moved to Milledgeville, to the Cline house in the center of town. At Peabody High School, Mary Flannery was lively as well as studious. She wrote and illustrated books, and in her senior year she listed her hobby in the yearbook as "Collecting rejection slips." Among other pets she had a quail named Amelia Earhart and a tame goose; she rode horseback and made masonite jewelry. In 1941 Edward O'Connor died. Mary Flannery graduated from high school the next year, and enrolled in the Women's College of Georgia (then the Georgia State College for Women) in Milledgeville.

At college Mary Flannery majored in English and social science; she was art editor of the newspaper, editor of the literary quarterly, and feature editor of the yearbook. She wrote fiction for the literary quarterly, *The Corinthian*, but she thought of herself primarily as a cartoonist. In her senior year she submitted cartoons to the *New Yorker*, which encouraged her but never bought any.

She was graduated with an A.B. in 1945. One of her English teachers had submitted some of her stories to the Writers' Workshop of the University of Iowa, and she was awarded a Rinehart Fellowship at the Workshop. She now came to think of herself primarily as a fiction writer. In Iowa City she worked hard at writing, and continued to send out stories. The first one that sold appeared in *Accent* in 1946. In June of 1947 she received the degree of Master of Fine Arts in Literature. She stayed on at the university for another year, then went to Yaddo, where she began her first novel, *Wise Blood*, and later moved to an apartment hotel in New York. Four chapters of *Wise Blood* were published in *Mademoiselle, Sewanee Review*, and *Partisan Review* in 1948 and 1949. In New York, she became friendly with two other literary Roman Catholics, Robert and Sally Fitzgerald. When they bought a house in Ridgefield, Connecticut, in the summer of 1949, she moved out with them as their boarder, all the while continuing to work on *Wise Blood*.

Late in 1950 Flannery O'Connor became very sick; in Atlanta her ailment was diagnosed as disseminated lupus. She was pulled through with blood transfusions, and the disease was arrested with injections of a cortisone derivative, ACTH, then in the experimental stage. When Miss O'Connor was released from the hospital in the summer of 1951, she was too weak to climb stairs, so she and her mother moved to Andalusia, a dairy farm a few miles outside Milledgeville. There Mrs. O'Connor managed the farm, and Miss O'Connor, when her health improved in the fall, went back to writing, in a ground-floor room.

Wise Blood had been accepted for publication by Harcourt, Brace while Miss O'Connor was in the hospital, and it was published in 1952, to a chorus of praise and misunderstanding by some reviewers, outrage and misunderstanding by others. The daily routine at Andalusia became fixed. Flannery wrote in the mornings, then her mother drove them into Milledgeville to have the excellent lunch at the Sanford House. In the afternoons and evenings, if there were no visitors, she watched the fowl on the farm, read, or painted. The massive doses of ACTH weakened her bones; eventually her hip bones would not bear her weight. She used a cane at first, then from 1955 on she got around on aluminum crutches with arm supports.

Milledgeville liked Flannery O'Connor and was proud of her, but tended not to read her work and to be shocked and dismayed by what it did read. At least at first, many of the townspeople resented her fiction as a mockery of the Baptist and Methodist faiths. If she wanted to make fun of religion, a number of them felt, she should write about her own religion and make fun of *it*.

She kept up an extensive correspondence with a great many people, some of whom she never met. Any crank could write her and get a reply. A few of her letters have been published since her death, and they show her to have been an eloquent if often whimsical correspondent. In the same anti-intellectual spirit in which she sent Uncle Remus postcards to friends, she slipped readily into a folksy idiom: "I have done forgot," "them interleckchuls," and such.

Although Miss O'Connor disliked travel, and her crutches made it difficult to get around, she accepted all the lecture invitations that she could, even if they paid little or nothing. She always read her lectures word for word, and it is clear, now that several of them have been published, that they were very carefully composed, that they say exactly what she meant to say in exactly the words in which she meant to say it.

The special quality of her verbal humor, always delivered dead-

7

pan, is hard to describe. Perhaps it was Irish, but if so it was the corrosive Irish wit of Stephen Dedalus and his father, not the be-jabers of stage Paddy. She took a sardonic pleasure in being pho-tographed, grim and unsmiling, against the unpainted and di-lapidated house of their Negro tenant farmers, and she remarked of the resulting photograph: "Looks like Sherman's just gone through." Of the Uncle Remus Museum in nearby Eatonton, the birthplace of Joel Chandler Harris, she said, "It's the only air-conditioned slave cabin in the United States." Of her trip to Lourdes: "I had the best-looking crutches in Europe." One year she gave her mother a jackass for Mother's Day, explaining it as "For the mother who has everything." She once told an interviewer that she always read "A Good Man Is Hard to Find" to college audiences because it was the only story of hers that she could read aloud "without busting out laughing."

A fair share of honors and awards came Flannery O'Connor's way during her lifetime. She received a Kenyon Review Fellow-ship in Fiction in 1953, and a renewal of it in 1954; a grant from the National Institute of Arts and Letters in 1957, and a grant from the Ford Foundation in 1959. Her stories won the O. Henry first prizes in 1957, 1963, and 1964. In 1962 she received an hon-orary D.Litt. from St. Mary's College, Notre Dame, and in 1963 a similar degree from Smith.

Early in 1964, while she was at work on an untitled third novel (a collection of stories, *A Good Man Is Hard to Find*, appeared in 1955; a second novel, *The Violent Bear It Away*, in 1960), Flan-nery O'Connor had to have an abdominal tumor removed. It proved benign, but the lupus became reactivated and her kid-neys were affected. Miss O'Connor knew she was dying. She hoped only to finish enough stories for a book. By a marvel of the will, she did. She died early on August 3, 1964. *Everything That Rises Must Converge* appeared posthumously in 1965.

Shortly after the publication of *The Violent Bear It Away,* Flannery O'Connor wrote to Sister Mariella Gable O.S.B., "I can wait fifty years, a hundred years, for it to be understood." Her reputation, here and abroad, was growing in the last years of her life, and has greatly increased since her death. *Wise Blood* was published in France (because of the dialect a feat of translation by Maurice Coindreau) and was received as an important Existentialist novel. So far, the growing acclaim has not been accompanied by any comparable understanding of her meanings and purposes. It is toward that end that the following pages modestly aspire.

Flannery O'Connor's first novel, *Wise Blood* (1952), is a tragicomic account of the making of an anchorite in our unlikely time. The young protagonist, Hazel Motes, called "Haze" (a haze in the eyes, a mote in the eyes, a beam in the eyes?), loses his faith while in the army, and becomes an apostle of negativism. He goes from his native Eastrod (the rood in the East?), Tennessee, to a city called "Taulkinham" that is obviously Atlanta, to preach the "church of truth without Jesus Christ Crucified." He wears a preacher's bright blue suit and a preacher's fierce black hat, but the only sign he gives of his power is a mysterious "Take your hand off me" to a policeman and a truckdriver (the *Noli me tangere* of the risen Christ in John's Gospel). As a result of Haze's refusal to go along with a religion-faker who calls himself Onnie Jay Holy (and is actually named Hoover Shoats), a man is hired to dress up as Haze and replace him, and Haze eventually murders the False Prophet, his *Doppelgänger.*

Another sort of antagonist is a boy named Enoch Emery, who works as a guard at the city park, and has his own religious mystery: in fixed ritual stages he must daily have a sacramental milkshake and make suggestive remarks to the waitress, then visit the

9

zoo animals and make obscene comments on their appearance, finally go to the museum and pay his devotions to a mummy. These are Enoch's Stations of the Cross, as we note from the pun I have italicized: "We got to *cross* this road and go down this hill. We got to go on foot," Enoch tells Haze, but he does not know why. Eventually Enoch steals the mummy, which he thinks of as "the new jesus," and presents it to Haze, who smashes it. Enoch also reads the comics "every evening like an office." Eventually he finds his religious fulfillment dressed in a stolen gorilla costume, but it is as the apostle of the mummified "new jesus" that he functions in Haze's pilgrim's progress.

There is still another false prophet, a fake blind man named Asa Hawks who pretends to have blinded himself with lime to justify his belief in Redemption. Haze puts Hawks in the role of Elijah in his new faith, and expects "a secret welcome" from him. What he gets instead is Hawks's homely little fifteen-year-old daughter Sabbath Lily, who moves into Haze's bed, becomes the Madonna of the new jesus (she cradles the mummy in her arms, and addresses Haze as its "daddy"), and eventually turns into a monster of sexual voracity and heartlessness. She calmly watches as Haze improves on her father by *really* blinding himself with lime, then she as calmly deserts him.

The other important character in the novel, far more than a property or a symbol, is a high old rat-colored Essex automobile that Haze buys after he moves out of the room of a whore named Leora Watts. The Essex is Haze's religious mystery: It is Woman (the salesman asks him "would you like to get under and look up it?"), Ordination (Haze preaches No Jesus from its hood, as his grandfather had preached Jesus from the hood of his car in Haze's childhood), and Redemption ("Nobody with a good car needs to be justified," Haze tells Sabbath Lily, in the book's most wonderful line). Haze kills the False Prophet by running over him with the Essex, which then leaves, in a kind of Calvary sweat, "little bead-chains of water and oil and gas on the road"; when a policeman gets the Essex off the road by the simple expedient of pushing it over an embankment, Haze is left with no place to go but an inner Calvary of blindness, asceticism, and sacrificial death at the hands of the police.

The techniques for unifying this garish and diverse material include a heavy reliance on symbolism. The principal symbol that unifies (along with the mummy and the Essex) is the "wise blood" of the title. Enoch knows things "by his blood," because "He had wise blood like his daddy." He protests to Haze: "You think you got wiser blood than anybody else." Of course Haze *thinks* he has wise blood — the blood of the natural body that is his only reality — and he preaches "the church that the blood of Jesus don't foul with redemption"; but Haze, in the author's view, really *has* wise blood: the blood of his grandfather, the inherited vocation, that preaches *through him* Christ's Blood, shed to redeem.

Haze's "church of truth without Jesus Christ Crucified" is not only a body of doctrine, it is an important symbol. Here are some of its more striking tenets: "I don't say he wasn't crucified but I say it wasn't for you"; "Jesus is a trick on niggers"; "There was no Fall because there was nothing to fall from and no Redemption because there was no Fall and no Judgment because there wasn't the first two. Nothing matters but that Jesus was a liar"; "I believe in a new kind of jesus . . . one that can't waste his blood redeeming people with it, because he's all man and ain't got any God in him"; "I preach the Church Without Christ, the church peaceful and satisfied!" This is wonderfully funny, and a sharp mockery of secular rationalism, but on another level it is desperately in earnest, an indictment of the smug and secular Church today. This is made clear by a sly joke in a conversation between Haze and his landlady about his Church Without Christ: " 'Protestant?' she asked suspiciously, 'or something foreign?' He said no mam, it was Protestant."

Two principal strands of covert symbolism affirm what Haze denies. One is the oaths the characters use unconsciously. "Good Jesus," Enoch says. "My Jesus," Haze mutters, or "Sweet Jesus Christ Crucified." Sabbath Lily's explanation of why she is abandoning Haze gives us the book's deepest meaning in a brilliant pun: "She said she hadn't counted on no honest-to-Jesus blind man." The other is the rock-strewn landscape. When he was ten, Haze's guilt at seeing a naked woman in a tent show and picturing his mother in her place had led him to punish himself by walking with "stones and small rocks" in his shoes. Out driving the Essex, he sees a boulder on which is painted a call to repentance and "Jesus Saves." Later we are told: "Hazel Motes's face might have been cut out of the side of a rock" in his indifference to Enoch, and he ends the scene by throwing a rock at Enoch. Haze's duffel bag contains a Bible "that had sat like a rock in the bottom of the bag for the last few years." Blinded and chastising his flesh at the end, he lines his shoes with "gravel and broken glass and pieces of small stone." Eventually we recognize these stones, rocks, and boulders: they are tokens of the Rock, Peter's Church.

As this covert symbolism suggests, the development of the action is elaborately foreshadowed. One such motif is the general denial of Haze's denial of his vocation (from the negation of the negation, a wisdom). Hawks says "I can hear the urge for Jesus in his voice" and tells him "Some preacher has left his mark on you"; and Sabbath Lily tells Haze retrospectively, "I seen you wouldn't never have no fun or let anybody else because you didn't want nothing but Jesus!"

Haze's self-blinding is even more elaborately foreshadowed in the imagery, starting with the name "Hazel Motes," which opens the novel. Haze dismisses Hawks as "a blind fool," and rhetorically asks the first audience to which he preaches: "Don't I have eyes in my head? Am I a blind man?" Enoch sees the reflection of Haze's eyes in the glass of the mummy case as "like two clean bullet holes." Sabbath Lily tells her father why she likes Haze's eyes: "They don't look like they see what he's looking at but they keep on looking." When Haze drives out into the country with Sabbath Lily, the sky has "only one cloud in it, a large blinding white one with curls and a beard" (perhaps a little too patly God the Father). Haze tells Sabbath that his Essex is so superior because "It was built by people with their eyes open that knew where they were at," and by way of comment, the First Person of God turns into the Third, the Holy Ghost: "The blinding white cloud had turned into a bird with long thin wings and was disappearing in the opposite direction."

After Haze blinds himself, his landlady thinks: "Why had he destroyed his eyes and saved himself unless he had some plan, unless he saw something that he couldn't get without being blind to everything else?" At the end of the book, the landlady recognizes that she needs Haze: "If she was going to be blind when she was dead, who better to guide her than a blind man? Who better to lead the blind than the blind, who knew what it was like?" When she next sees him, he has been clubbed to death by the police. The landlady looks into his eyes "and the deep burned eye sockets seemed to lead into the dark tunnel where he had disappeared." As she stares, with her eyes shut, she sees him "moving farther and farther away, farther and farther into the darkness until he was the pin point of light" (this pinpoint of light had earlier been identified as the star over Bethlehem). Haze has been advancing "backwards to Bethlehem," in her words, and he has finally arrived there.

The organization of *Wise Blood* is thus a tight network of imagery, symbolism, and foreshadowing. The plot of the novel is

13

much less tight, since the whole episode of Enoch and the gorilla suit is unrelated to Haze, and Enoch simply falls out of the book dressed as a gorilla. The language similarly shows that Miss O'Connor had not reached the stage of full control of her material. Some of it represents the perfect plain style of her later triumphs, but some of the tropes are so garish or elaborate as to be distracting, and thus ineffective. At one point, for example, Haze's face looks "like one of those closet doors in gangster pictures where someone is tied to a chair behind it with a towel in his mouth."

Perhaps the most remarkable thing about *Wise Blood*, in comparison with the later fiction, is its pervasive sexuality. Enoch prays to Jesus to help him escape from the woman who adopted him, and Jesus' answer to the prayer is the use of sex as aggression: "I went in her room without my pants on and pulled the sheet off her and giver a heart attact." The zoo animals that Enoch has to observe as a station of his cross represent sex as shameful: "If I had a ass like that," Enoch says prudishly of an ape, "I'd sit on it. I wouldn't be exposing it to all these people come to this park." One of the events that lead Haze to seduce Sabbath Lily involves sex as ludicrous: Leora Watts gets up one night while he is asleep and cuts "the top of his hat out in an obscene shape." Haze's sexual attachments in the novel are deeply perverse: a corrupt mother, a corrupt child, and an old Essex.

Wise Blood has been much misunderstood. If anything, the confusion was deepened in 1957, when the author printed her first public statement of her intentions, the essay "The Fiction Writer and His Country" in Granville Hicks's symposium *The Living Novel*. In it Miss O'Connor writes: "For I am no disbeliever in spiritual purpose and no vague believer. I see from the standpoint of Christian orthodoxy. This means that for me the meaning of life is centered in our Redemption by Christ and that what I see in the world I see in its relation to that." Her intentions were more specifically clarified in the tiny Author's Note to the second edition of *Wise Blood* in 1962, in which she describes the work as "a comic novel about a Christian *malgré lui,* and as such, very serious."

The problem is that the novel's Christian themes are put paradoxically, even negatively, the way Haze progresses to Bethlehem. One is Original Sin. In the army, Haze wants to lose his faith because he wants to escape from the knowledge of his fallen nature, "to be converted to nothing instead of to evil." He tells Hawks, "If I was in sin I was in it before I ever committed any," and he tells a waitress, "If Jesus existed, I wouldn't be clean." Another important theme is Affirmation by Blasphemy. Haze tells his sidewalk audience, "The only way to the truth is through blasphemy," and he reaffirms this doctrine against Onnie Jay Holy's principle, "If you want to get anywheres in religion, you got to keep it sweet." Haze later tells a boy at a filling station that "he had only a few days ago believed in blasphemy as the way to salvation, but that you couldn't even believe in that because then you were believing in something to blaspheme."

A third Christian theme of *Wise Blood* is Vocation. The landlady thinks of Haze, after he is blind, "He might as well be one of them monks . . . he might as well be in a monkery." Haze throws away his leftover money each month; he puts rocks in his shoes, and when the landlady asks him why, he says, "To pay," but he does not tell her what he is paying *for,* and it seems unlikely that he knows. When she discovers that he wears barbed wire around his chest, she tells him, "People have quit doing it." "They ain't quit doing it as long as I'm doing it," Haze answers. It is clear that he has founded a private monastic order, ascetic and penitential, and that the truth he formerly preached negatively he now witnesses to mutely, and will be martyred for. With no institution to channel its violence, in Miss O'Connor's view, his call can only destroy him.

15

Of the ten stories of *A Good Man Is Hard to Find* (1955), the three best, in my opinion, are "The Artificial Nigger," "Good Country People," and "The Displaced Person." "The Artificial Nigger" was Miss O'Connor's own favorite, and it makes impressive claims to be considered her best story. It tells of two backwoods Georgians, an old man named Mr. Head and his grandson Nelson, who go to the terrifying city for Nelson's first visit. The action of the story is their estrangement and reconciliation, but it is a readjustment as profound as that of the Conroys of Joyce's "The Dead." Nelson has never seen a Negro before, and the preliminary events of the story are encounters with real Negroes — first a huge Negro man on the train, wearing a yellow satin tie with a ruby stickpin, then an enormous Negro woman they meet on the street, whom Nelson inexplicably wants to hold him and mother him.

The dramatic crisis in the story is Nelson's running into an elderly white woman on the street, knocking her down and scattering her groceries. Mr. Head panics and re-enacts Peter's denial: " 'This is not my boy,' he said, 'I never seen him before.' " Nelson's subsequent hatred and contempt, and Mr. Head's guilt and shame, are wonderfully funny and moving, profoundly true and beautiful. Their reconciliation comes when they see, decorating a lawn, a shabby plaster statue of a Negro eating a watermelon. In the same voice, each exclaims: "An artificial nigger!" This communion transforms them magically, and they exchange identities: "Mr. Head looked like an ancient child and Nelson like a miniature old man." The artificial Negro is God's grace: "They could both feel it dissolving their differences like an action of mercy." Mr. Head has a moment of true repentance and charity, he and the boy are united in love, and the story is over.

The protagonist of "Good Country People" is the author's cruelest self-caricature: Joy Hopewell, hulking, thirty-two, a learned

Doctor of Philosophy. She has an artificial leg as a result of a hunting accident, she has changed her name legally from Joy to Hulga, she wears a yellow sweat shirt with a picture of a cowboy on a horse, and she is an atheist. When a simple-seeming country boy appears selling Bibles, she sets out to seduce him, and she appears for their date (in a perfect touch) wearing Vapex on the collar of her shirt, "since she did not own any perfume."

The Bible salesman appears to be another Hazel Motes, wearing the same bright blue suit and wide-brimmed hat, and protesting "I'm just a country boy." He turns out to be the False Prophet instead: when they are alone in the barn loft he reveals that his hollow Bible contains a flask of whiskey, a pack of pornographic playing cards, and a package of condoms. "You ain't so smart," he tells Joy-Hulga as he disappears down the loft trapdoor with her artificial leg, "I been believing in nothing ever since I was born!" It is the exposure of a fake Christian, but more significantly it is the exposure of a fake atheist, her intellectual pride and superiority revealed to be only ignorance and gullibility. Unfortunately, the story does not end where it should, with the symbolic defloration of the theft of the leg and the Bible salesman's reproof, but goes on for two paragraphs of superfluous irony.

"The Displaced Person" is the longest and most ambitious story in the book. In it a Polish Catholic refugee, Mr. Guizac, comes to work for Protestant Mrs. McIntyre, a widow who runs a dairy farm. He is the displaced person, but in the course of the complex tragic action, Mr. Shortley, the native hired man, becomes a displaced person when Mrs. McIntyre fires him, Mrs. Shortley becomes a displaced person when she dies of a stroke as they depart, Mr. Guizac becomes further displaced when the rehired Mr. Shortley carelessly allows a tractor to run over his spine, and Mrs. McIntyre herself becomes a displaced person at the end, collapsed, bedridden, and alone.

17

None of these melodramatic events, however, is the significant action of the story. The central figure in the story is a peacock, who enters in the first sentence, following Mrs. Shortley up the road, and exits in the last, when the priest feeds him breadcrumbs on his weekly visit to instruct the bedridden Mrs. McIntyre in the doctrines of his Church. The peacock is a traditional symbol of Christ's divinity and the Resurrection. In the story he functions as a kind of spiritual test: Mrs. Shortley never notices him; Mrs. McIntyre sees him only as "another mouth to feed"; her husband the late Judge had kept peacocks because "they made him feel rich"; the priest is overwhelmed by the peacock's beauty, and says of the spread tail, "Christ will come like that!"

As the peacock symbolizes Christ's divine nature, so the displaced person symbolizes His human nature. In the story's key conversation, Mrs. McIntyre says, in reference to Mr. Guizac, "He didn't have to come in the first place," and the absentminded old priest, mistaking her reference, answers, "He came to redeem us." Later, annoyed with all the religious talk, Mrs. McIntyre says indignantly to the priest, "As far as I'm concerned, Christ was just another D. P." But Mr. Guizac does more than embody Christ as he is displaced, suffers, and is slain. "That man is my salvation," Mrs. McIntyre had said earlier, in praise of Mr. Guizac's hard work, and the remark has Miss O'Connor's usual double meaning. "I am not responsible for the world's misery," Mrs. McIntyre tells Mr. Guizac later. But his death, in which they are all equally guilty, is redemptive for her insofar as it abases her pride and prepares her to accept the burden of the world's misery.

The other stories in the book are less impressive. The title story, "A Good Man Is Hard to Find," is a melodrama about a family casually wiped out by an escaped criminal called the Misfit, and in spots it is cruelly funny. "The River" is about a young boy who finds a symbolic baptism in drowning. Like *Wise Blood*, it relies heavily on the ironic use of profanity: "Well then for Christ's sake fix him," Harry's father says to the woman taking care of him, who does just that; "Healed of what for Christ's sake?" Harry's mother asks, unaware that the question contains its answer. The story is a little too pat, however, and the empty secular life of the parents is an unconvincing travesty. "The Life You Save May Be Your Own" is a slice of Tobacco Road, redeemed by Mr. Shiftlet's automobilolatry (the car represents an ideal marriage to him, as to Hazel Motes, and his destination is significantly "Mobile") and by a superb comic ending.

"A Stroke of Good Fortune" is the one markedly unsuccessful story in the book, a leaden tract against complacency and contraception. "A Temple of the Holy Ghost" is a portrait of the artist as a sardonic twelve-year-old girl, a Roman Catholic among rustics who identify Latin hymns as "Jew singing." "A Circle in the Fire" does not quite bring off its terror, but it has one moment of magnificent empathy, when the young girl sees the naked boys bathing in the woods, and thinks, not of how they look, but of how they *see*: "The trees must have looked like green waterfalls through his wet glasses." It is just this empathy that is lacking at the end, when she looks at her mother's face and sees it "as if it might have belonged to anybody, a Negro or a European or to Powell himself." Mrs. Cope has become a displaced person like Mrs. McIntyre, but she is never seen from inside as the boy Powell is. The remaining story, "A Late Encounter with the Enemy," is sharply satiric, of the deviled corsages of Hollywood as of the South's Confederacy cult, but it rises to distinction only in the incongruous final tableau: the old general's corpse sitting in the Coca-Cola line.

Her second novel, *The Violent Bear It Away* (1960), is Miss O'Connor's masterpiece. It tells the terrible initiation of a reluctant prophet. The adolescent protagonist is Francis Marion

Tarwater (his name is as richly symbolic as Hazel Motes's: Francis Marion is the "old swamp fox" of the Revolutionary War, tarwater is a discredited folk cure-all). He is recognizable by the author's usual sign of election, Jesus' *Noli me tangere*, early in the book. When the old Negro, Buford Munson, finds young Tarwater drunk and his great-uncle dead, Buford says, "He was deep in Jesus' misery," and young Tarwater replies, "Nigger . . . take your hand off me." The great-uncle, Mason Tarwater, was a mad prophet who made his living distilling bootleg whiskey, and kept "worthless black game bantams" as the old Judge kept worthless peacocks. The secular antagonist, George F. Rayber (raper?), young Tarwater's uncle and old Tarwater's nephew, is an ambiguous figure. He is Satanic, taking on, "like the devil," any look that suited him, but he is a *monk* of Satan, controlling the family curse of violence and madness in his blood ("he was the stuff of which fanatics and madmen are made") by "a rigid ascetic discipline," by rationality and good works. His mad barefoot pursuit of young Tarwater through the streets of the town is a penitential pilgrimage; more than Tarwater, *Rayber* looks "like a fanatical country preacher," and young Tarwater tells him perceptively (my italics): "It's *you* the seed fell in."

Rayber's idiot son, Bishop, is less a character than a sacrament: young Tarwater has been commanded by his great-uncle to begin his ministry by baptizing Bishop, and when he has the opportunity he compulsively baptizes and drowns him. The novel's other important character is Satan. He first appears as a skeptical voice in young Tarwater's drunken head, then as a vision of a friendly stranger in a panama hat; he returns as a voice to direct the drowning of Bishop; he appears in the flesh at the end of the novel to drug and rape young Tarwater in the final stage of his initiation into deranged prophecy.

The Violent, like *Wise Blood*, is tightly unified by symbolism.

The principal unifying symbol is burning. Evils "come from the Lord and burn the prophet clean," old Tarwater had told the boy; "even the mercy of the Lord burns." Young Tarwater imagines his return to the city after he receives his prophetic call, when "he would return with fire in his eyes." Old Tarwater once wrote a warning to Rayber: "THE PROPHET I RAISE UP OUT OF THIS BOY WILL BURN YOUR EYES CLEAN." After the old man's death, Tarwater burns their shack, intending to cremate the corpse in defiance of old Tarwater's fervent wish to be buried to await the Resurrection. On his way to the city, young Tarwater takes the glow of its lights to be the fire he set (a foreshadowing of his eventual return as a prophet). His eyes appear to Rayber to be "singed with guilt." (They foreshadow his madness, as Haze's eyes foreshadow his blindness.) A girl evangelist challenges Rayber as a damned soul and says, "The Word of God is a burning Word to burn you clean!" Young Tarwater burns himself clean in a secular sense after the rape by firing the woods where it occurred, but he has been burned clean in his great-uncle's sense too: his "scorched eyes" now look "as if, touched with a coal like the lips of the prophet, they would never be used for ordinary sights again." He then sets fire to his own woods, sees the fire he has set as the expected sign over his great-uncle's grave, "the burning bush," and hears God's command: "GO WARN THE CHILDREN OF GOD OF THE TERRIBLE SPEED OF MERCY." He sets his "singed eyes," in the book's last sentence, "toward the dark city, where the children of God lay sleeping." He is finally a prophet, and a madman.

A second important symbol, balancing judgment with mercy, is spiritual feeding. When old Tarwater got into his coffin to try it on for size, the boy saw "nothing showing but his stomach which rose over the top like over-leavened bread." The bread symbolized by the old man's belly is "the bread of life," Jesus, and young Tarwater decides that he is "not hungry for the bread of life." But when Rayber, in pursuing him through the city, sees him staring obsessively at a loaf of bread in a bakery window, Rayber thinks characteristically, "If he had eaten his dinner, he wouldn't be hungry." Young Tarwater tells a truckdriver who gives him a lift that he is hungry for real food; "I ain't hungry for the bread of life." Later he drinks the stranger's drugged liquor and remarks: "It's better than the Bread of Life!" Standing over his great-uncle's grave at the end, he has a vision of Mason Tarwater on the banks of the Lake of Galilee, eating the multiplied loaves and fishes, and he is "aware at last of the object of his hunger, aware that it was the same as the old man's and that nothing on earth would fill him." (As the old man's belly is the bread, his eyes are the fishes: "silver protruding eyes that looked like two fish straining to get out of a net of red threads"; "mad fish-colored eyes.")

The other important symbol in *The Violent Bear It Away* is Bishop, the holy idiot. Bishop's habitual toy is a trashbasket with a rock in it. He is able to make peanut butter sandwiches "though sometimes he put the bread inside." At one point Rayber realizes that young Tarwater is looking at Bishop but seeing "only a spot of light." These are all symbols we have noted before: Peter's Rock, the living Bread, the Star of Bethlehem. The woman who runs the resort where the murderous baptism occurs makes Bishop's sacramental nature explicit. When Tarwater drives Bishop away for touching him, she reproves Tarwater, "Mind how you talk to one of them there," and glares at him fiercely, "as if he had profaned the holy."

The structure of foreshadowing is more economical than that of *Wise Blood* and no less effective. Old Tarwater had warned his grand-nephew of the special dangers incurred by prophets: " 'You are the kind of boy,' the old man said, 'that the devil is always going to be offering to assist, to give you a smoke or a drink or a ride, and to ask you your bidnis. You had better mind how you take up with strangers.' " A salesman predicts of Tarwater, "He won't come to no good end." Rayber takes Tarwater back to Tennessee because "He saw no way of curing him except perhaps through some shock." Everything unfolds as prophesied: the devil gives Tarwater a ride, the shock cures, the cure is a no good end, at least in the world's eyes. Unlike that of *Wise Blood*, the narrative structure of *The Violent* is perfectly shaped; there are no loose ends like Enoch Emery. Here is *The Violent*'s magnificent first sentence: "Francis Marion Tarwater's uncle had been dead for only half a day when the boy got too drunk to finish digging his grave and a Negro named Buford Munson, who had come to get a jug filled, had to finish it and drag the body from the breakfast table where it was still sitting and bury it in a decent and Christian way, with the sign of its Saviour at the head of the grave and enough dirt on top to keep the dogs from digging it up." The novel unfolds the motifs of the opening sentence inexorably, from this first drunkenness to the final drugged drunkenness and transformation. Even the sodomic rape, not much appreciated by the reviewers, is right and inevitable: it is at once the ultimate violation of the untouchable anointed of the Lord, a naturalistic explanation for the shaman's spirit possession, and a shocking and effective metaphor for seizure by divine purpose. (Yeats makes a similar use of rape in "Leda and the Swan.")

The book's language is sparse and functional. Old Tarwater's instructions for his burial read like the best Twain ("Get two boards and set them down the steps and start me rolling and dig where I stop and don't let me roll over into it until it's deep enough"). The tropes, however imaginative, are for the most part economical and functional; for example, "The words were as silent as seeds opening one at a time in his blood." Even a few far-fetched ones, such as Rayber's eyes looking "like something human trapped in a switch box," seem to justify themselves.

Finally there is the problem of the book's meaning. The chief clue is the title epigraph, Matthew 11:12, printed in very large type across the double title page: "From the days of John the Baptist until now, the kingdom of heaven suffereth violence, and the violent bear it away." This has been widely misinterpreted. The Authorized Version translates the last clause "and the violent take it by force," and the New English Bible reads "and violent men are seizing it." Its clear meaning is that the violent are enemies of the kingdom, capturing it from the righteous, as a sign of the imminent coming of the Messiah, the Christ. In this sense the Tarwaters are mad fanatics carrying away the kingdom from its lukewarm heirs, and Rayber is an equally mad fanatic preaching secular salvation. Rayber sees himself "divided in two — a violent and a rational self." Violence and madness are the curse in the family's blood, but Rayber succeeds in controlling them. The effect of the novel's events on young Tarwater is to extirpate the rational self instead, to burn away all reason and leave him entirely violent and mad.

It is in this extreme sense that young Tarwater is an allegory of the Church, which must lose the world to save it. Where *Wise Blood* is about Vocation along with several other mysteries, *The Violent* is wholly and centrally about Vocation and the prophet's necessary stage of resistance to Vocation (from Moses' pleading his speech defect to Jonah's taking flight). When old Tarwater said that if he died without baptizing Bishop, the baptism of Bishop would be "the first mission the Lord sends you," "the boy doubted very much that his first mission would be to baptize a dim-witted child." When his great-uncle tells of their freedom, young Tarwater feels "a slow warm rising resentment that this freedom had to be connected with Jesus and that Jesus had to be the Lord."

The analogy with Bible prophets is made again and again: "The old man compared their situation to that of Elijah and Elisha";

persecuted by Rayber, the old man is simultaneously "Jonah, Ezekiel, Daniel, he was at that moment all of them — the swallowed, the lowered, the enclosed"; arriving at Rayber's house, young Tarwater is similarly transformed: "His whole body felt hollow as if he had been lifted like Habakkuk by the hair of his head, borne swiftly through the night and set down in the place of his mission." When young Tarwater realizes his mission regarding Bishop, "He did not look into the eyes of any fiery beast or see a burning bush. He only knew, with a certainty sunk in despair, that he was expected to baptize the child he saw and begin the life his great-uncle had prepared him for."

In the book's boldest image, repeated after the drowning of Bishop, young Tarwater pictures himself "trudging into the distance in the bleeding stinking mad shadow of Jesus." He tirelessly insists to Rayber, of his great-uncle, "He ain't had no effect on me." The stranger's voice assures young Tarwater that he has not been called or received a sign, that all he feels are sensations, whereas Jonah's three days in the belly of the fish, "That was a sign; it wasn't no sensation." "The Lord speaks to prophets personally," the stranger adds, "and He's never spoke to you." But slowly, relentlessly, through denial and burning, murder and rape, Tarwater hears his call and responds, and in his madness he will preach the truth. Man is both vessel and instrument of divine purpose, and divine purpose is not answerable to human reason.

In *Everything That Rises Must Converge* (1965), the finest of the stories, to my taste, and the one least like anything Miss O'Connor (or anyone else) has done before, is "Parker's Back," the last story she wrote before her death. It tells of a young man named O. E. Parker whose only distinction is a passion for having himself elaborately tattooed. In what he believes is an accommodation to his wife's Fundamentalist piety, Parker has a Byzantine mosaic of a staring Christ reproduced on his back. He is then literally *christophoros*, Christ-bearing, "witnessing for Jesus" on his hide. Under this coloration Parker is transformed and reborn, resuming the Old Testament prophet names, Obadiah Elihue, that he has always concealed behind his initials, and suffering a Punch and Judy martyrdom as he passively allows his wife to punish his "idolatry" by beating him with a broom until "large welts had formed on the face of the tattooed Christ." The story is simultaneously uproarious and deeply moving, and the metaphor of tattooing — bloody, painful, indelible; garish, out of fashion, ludicrous — for the burden of Redemption is uncanny and perfect, a truly metaphysical conceit.

A long and ambitious story, "The Lame Shall Enter First," is impressive in a more familiar fashion. It is another look at the trio of Rayber, Bishop, and young Tarwater (in fact, according to Robert Fitzgerald's introduction to *Everything That Rises*, it uses material cut from *The Violent*). Superficially, the story is pathetic sociology: a well-meaning but unimaginative widower, Sheppard, neglects his son Norton, mainly because an older boy, Rufus Johnson, clubfooted and criminal, seems much more in need of help; the consequence is Norton's suicide. On a more perceptive level, Rufus is not a poor deprived cripple, but evil, demonic, a type of Satan; and Sheppard learns the reality of these entities to his cost. (This is Fitzgerald's reading in the introduction, encouraged by the statement in the story that finally Sheppard "saw the clear-eyed Devil, the sounder of hearts, leering at him from the eyes of Johnson.") But this is Sheppard's interpretation, not the author's. Miss O'Connor's own reading, I believe, is consistent with her radical Christian dualism and far more challenging: not Rufus but *Sheppard* is the type of Satan, taking over God's prerogatives in His assumed absence; and Rufus is the true prophetic voice of Judgment, saying of Sheppard "He thinks he's Jesus Christ!" and challenging him, "Satan has you in his power." (This is the reading of Sister Rose Alice, in "Flannery O'Connor: Poet to the Outcast," in which she paraphrases the story's action as "The repulsive good defeats the urbane evil.")

The third triumph in the book is "The Enduring Chill," a devastatingly funny, if ultimately serious, story of a pretentious young man whose dramatic coming home to die turns out badly. The story mows down its targets with general ruthlessness: the Church is wickedly satirized in a scatterbrained and irascible old priest, blind in one eye and deaf in one ear; such secular "experience of communion" as racial integration comes off no better. The symbols are masterly. When Asbury, the romantic invalid, turns his head away in irritation from his mother's talk about the dairy herd, he confronts "a small, wall-eyed Guernsey . . . watching him steadily as if she sensed some bond between them." When he gets up to his room, there is a water stain on the ceiling that looks like "a fierce bird with spread wings," with "an icicle crosswise in his beak." In the comic ending, the bond between Asbury and the wall-eyed Guernsey is the discovery, by the local doctor Asbury despises, that his supposedly fatal disease is only undulant fever, caught from drinking unpasteurized milk; in the apocalyptic ending that follows the comedy, the fierce bird on the ceiling is discovered to be the Holy Ghost, "emblazoned in ice instead of fire," and, implacably, that terribly swift mercy descends upon him.

The other stories are less impressive or are flawed in some fashion. The title story, "Everything That Rises Must Converge," has a fine ending, Julian's "entry into the world of guilt and sorrow" when his mother has a stroke occasioned by a Negro woman who rose and converged with her. It is beautifully foreshadowed from the story's first sentence, but the characters, a travesty segregationist mother and a travesty integrationist son, are not adequate to the finely structured action. "Greenleaf" takes another look at the widow running a dairy farm. Here she is Mrs. May, "a good Christian woman with a large respect for religion, though she did not, of course, believe any of it was true." Her punishment is undergoing a rather Freudian Dionysiac mystery in which a scrub bull, "like some patient god come down to woo her," gores her to death "like a wild tormented lover." Unfortunately, the two worlds of Bacchic ecstasy and regional satire in the story coexist uneasily. "A View of the Woods" is a perfect comic story about a conflict between a grandfather and a nine-year-old granddaughter just like him, up to its natural ending after the first paragraph on page 80; then it falls into the unnecessary multiple death of Jacobean drama. The melodramatic "The Comforts of Home" travesties Miss O'Connor's familiar triad of parent-child-intruder, and is the one story in the book that seems to me a mistake from the beginning. "Revelation" is a marvelously funny apocalypse for the Laodiceans that goes on too long. "Judgement Day" is a reworking, shortly before Miss O'Connor's death, of an old story first written at Iowa in 1946, and is thus the only story in the book set outside Georgia. It is a magical and compelling account of the death and symbolic resurrection of an old Georgia man in New York City, made resonant by the author's sense of her own imminent death; only the Negro characters in it (perhaps part of the early material) fail to ring true.

In all her writing, Flannery O'Connor has certain preoccupations that seem almost obsessional. A few simple images recur so strikingly that every reader notices them: the flaming suns, the mutilated eyes, the "Jesus-seeing" hats, the colorful shirts. These images may be obsessive with the author, but they are used organically in the fiction. The sun in "A Circle in the Fire" is a symbol and specific foreshadowing of the boys' incendiary threat: "It was swollen and flame-colored and hung in a net of ragged cloud as if it might burn through any second and fall into the woods." The sunset in "Greenleaf" is another "swollen red ball," but as Mrs. May watches, "it began to narrow and pale until it looked like a bullet." It is narrow and pale to resemble the moon, since the bull first appeared to woo Mrs. May "silvered in the moonlight"; it looks like a bullet because the bull will soon come like a streak to penetrate her body, bull-bullet indeed.

A few recurrent symbols are more complex than these. One is the young preacher in bright blue suit and stern black hat. His principal embodiments are Hazel Motes and the False Prophet in *Wise Blood*, and the Bible salesman in "Good Country People," but we see traces of him everywhere: the bright blue suit on the preacher who introduces the girl evangelist who tells Rayber that he is a damned soul in *The Violent*; the stern black hat on the old man in "Judgement Day." These are not simply a uniform, but emblems: the blue suit glares with raw Fundamentalist fervor, the black hat represents what the old man's daughter dismisses as "a lot of hardshell Baptist hooey." The False Prophet dresses like Haze to steal his mission, but as a consequence of the transformation he dies an exemplary Christian death, confessing his sins and calling out "Jesus hep me"; the Bible salesman disguises himself to cheat the gullible, but instead he is instrumental in bringing Joy-Hulga to the beginnings of humility in humiliation.

The peacock is another complex symbol. It is central in "The Displaced Person," but it appears in many places: the innocent deaf girl in "The Life You Save May Be Your Own" has "eyes as blue as a peacock's neck," and learns to say only one word, "bird"; Joy-Hulga is "as sensitive about the artificial leg as a peacock about his tail"; the little girl in *The Violent* preaches "Silver and gold and peacock tails, a thousand suns in a peacock's tail," and Rayber thinks of her as "one of those birds blinded to make it sing more sweetly." As the peacock was a personal image of the Second Coming for the old priest and of wealth for the old Judge in "The Displaced Person," so it seems to have been a personal image of freedom and beauty (that is, of *art*) for Miss O'Connor. In an article, "Living with a Peacock," in *Holiday*, Miss O'Connor wrote: "My frenzy said: I want so many of them that every time I go out the door I'll run into one." Of this abundance, which in another aspect is God's grace, the deaf girl has only the useless beauty, Joy-Hulga only the vulnerability.

Another complex symbol can only be called, in acknowledgment of Miss O'Connor's debt, Georgia Snopesism. It is principally embodied in two families, the Shortleys in "The Displaced Person" and the Greenleafs in "Greenleaf," but there is more than a touch of it in the Pritchards in "A Circle in the Fire" and the Freemans who are the "good country people" of the story of that title. These families of tenant farmers usually include a man who is stupid, incompetent, and malevolent; a wife with "a special fondness for the details of secret infections, hidden deformities, assaults upon children"; and two or more mindless and voracious children. More than any other figures in Miss O'Connor's work, these Snopes families are social, even class, symbols (as are their Mississippi counterparts in Faulkner). They represent the southern poor white class seen as intrinsically vicious. In the stories, they murder Mr. Guizac and let the bull gore Mrs. May; in our newspapers, they have other victims.

As this suggests, not only do images and symbols recur, but fixed groupings of people recur, and certain figures in these fixed groups are consistently travestied. Fitzgerald's introduction to *Everything That Rises* refers to what he calls the "family resemblance" shown by many of the characters in the stories and novels, but this is less a matter of recurrent figures than of recurrent relationships. One is the duo of practical mother and dreamy child on a dairy farm. In "A Circle in the Fire" they are a "very small and trim" woman and a "pale fat girl of twelve"; in "Good Country People" they are a mother who "had no bad qualities of her own but she was able to use other people's in such a constructive way that she never felt the lack," and Joy-Hulga; and so on. This mother and daughter are complementary in a curious fashion: each is caricatured as seen by the other, the resourceful widow as smug and empty, the arty child as useless and affected. In the later stories of *Everything That Rises*, this pairing is varied. Mrs. May in "Greenleaf" has two sons, of whom only the younger is an intellectual, although the older manages to be equally unsatisfactory: he sells insurance, but it is "the kind that only Negroes buy." Mrs. Fox in "The Enduring Chill" similarly has two children, who between them compose the familiar character: Asbury has the artistic pretensions, his sister Mary George the scathing tongue. This last splitting is repeated in the fragment of the unfinished novel published in *Esquire* as "Why Do the Heathens Rage?"

A relationship that does not involve mutual travesty is one between a boy and his mother's brother or father. The first of these is Haze and his grandfather, the circuit preacher. In "The Artificial Nigger" this pair becomes Mr. Head and his daughter's son Nelson; in *The Violent* we get the complexity of young Tarwater and his mother's brother Rayber, Rayber and *his* mother's brother old Tarwater, with the two Tarwaters in the duplicated magical relation of mother's brother of a mother's brother to sister's son of a sister's son. In "A View of the Woods," the pairing becomes mother's father and *girl*. In "The Lame Shall Enter First," Rufus Johnson lives with his crazy grandfather (presumably his mother's father), until the old man goes off "with a remnant to the hills," to prepare against the destruction of the world by fiery flood. The point of this relationship is that the grandfather or uncle is the true father, and the grandson or nephew (however he resists it) is the true heir. This replacement of the father as authority by the mother's brother or father would be natural enough in the writing of an author whose father died in her childhood, but before settling for an autobiographical cause here we should notice that the mother's brother rather than the father as family authority is an important feature of primitive matriliny, and thus of much of our most resonant myth and legend.

The third set of characters is the trio of parent, child, and wolf cub, first exemplified by Rayber, Bishop, and young Tarwater in *The Violent*. We see it again in "The Lame Shall Enter First," with Sheppard, Norton, and Rufus Johnson, and less satisfactorily in "The Comforts of Home," with Thomas' mother, Thomas, and Star, the nymphomaniac girl the mother brings home. Travesty consistently accompanies this grouping, too, but here parent and child do not judge each other, but are both judged harshly by the outsider. Through Tarwater's eyes, we see Rayber as a blind fool and Bishop as a worthless idiot; through Rufus' eyes we see Sheppard as a blasphemous do-gooder and Norton as a spiritless nonentity. This is not so neat in "The Comforts of Home," since "Star Drake" is too preposterous a character to judge anyone; essentially, there we see the absurd gullibility of Thomas' mother's absolute faith in human goodness through his eyes, and we similarly reject Thomas' absolute lack of charity as evidenced by his behavior.

Half a dozen important themes run through all Miss O'Connor's work. One is a profound equation of the mysteries of sex and religion. When young Hazel Motes sees the naked woman at the carnival, his mother tells him "Jesus died to redeem you" as she switches him, and the two guilty mysteries merge inextricably in his mind. As the title of "A Temple of the Holy Ghost" (a Christian metaphor for the body) makes clear, the story is centrally concerned with this equation. The twelve-year-old girl protagonist is initiated into sexual mystery by her older cousins, who tell her of the hermaphrodite they saw at the carnival; at the time she imagines herself a Christian martyr in a Roman a when the sun goes down "like an elevated Host drenched in blood to end the story, it is the blood of menstruation and childbirth as well as of martyrdom and Christ's Passion. The neatest of these sex-religion equations is Mrs. McIntyre's reaction, in "The Displaced Person," to the priest's own equation of Christ and the peacock's tail: "Mrs. McIntyre's face assumed a set puritanical expression and she reddened. Christ in the conversation embarrassed her the way sex had her mother."

Another recurrent theme is change of identity, transformation, death-and-rebirth. Parker in "Parker's Back" is transformed by the tattoo, but most often in the fiction transformation occurs by renaming. Harry Ashfield becomes Bevel, who counts, in "The River"; Joy chooses a way of life by becoming Hulga in "Good Country People"; Hoover Shoats transforms himself into Onnie Jay Holy to run a fake religious radio program called "Soulsease"; Rayber tries to remake young Tarwater by calling him "Frankie"; even Parker needs a baptismal name change from O. E. to Obadiah Elihue to be fully transformed.

A theme of great power in the work is what might be called the perverse mother. When Leora Watts first goes to bed with Hazel Motes, she tickles his chin "in a motherly way," calls him "son," and calls herself "Momma." The mummy in the novel is not only a mock Christ child but a pun on "mommy," as a Freudian would guess from its place as the ultimate revelation of Enoch's Mystery cult. (This guess is supported in "Everything That Rises Must Converge" by Julian's picture of his mother, "shrunken to the dwarf-like proportions of her moral nature, sitting like a mummy.") Here are Joy-Hulga and the Bible salesman seducing each other in the barn loft: "His breath was clear and sweet like a child's and the kisses were sticky like a child's. He mumbled about loving

33

her and about knowing when he first seen her that he loved her, but the mumbling was like the sleepy fretting of a child being put to sleep by his mother." Norton in "The Lame Shall Enter First" finds his dead mother in the sky through a telescope, but the only mother he finds in reality is death by hanging. Parker's mother "would not pay for any tattoo except her name on a heart, which he had put on, grumbling." Tarwater's mother, like Rayber's, was a whore, or so both Tarwaters are pleased to affirm.

Miss O'Connor's principal theme is what Walter Allen in *Esprit* excellently calls "a world of the God-intoxicated," pointing out that Rayber in his denial is as much intoxicated by God as are the Tarwaters. Miss O'Connor's male characters are God-intoxicated in a variety of ways. Those who have found their calling as preachers articulate the author's radical dualism. The preacher in "The River" challenges: "Believe Jesus or the devil! . . . Testify to one or the other!" Old Tarwater (and, we assume, Haze's grandfather) similarly rejects everything not Christ as anti-Christ. We see a youthful version of this figure in Rufus Johnson. Rejecting salvation from Sheppard, Rufus hisses: "Nobody can save me but Jesus." "If I do repent, I'll be a preacher," he says. "If you're going to do it, it's no sense in doing it half way." Sheppard sees him as "a small black figure on the threshold of some dark apocalypse." Rufus may continue to choose the devil, as Haze tried to do, or he may yet accept the call, as young Tarwater eventually does. The mark of election, the *Noli me tangere*, is on all three, but they are free to choose whether to preach the Word or, like Parker, mutely to witness it on their flesh.

One way that intoxication with God expresses itself, in short, is Satanism. The Misfit in "A Good Man Is Hard to Find" is a ruthless killer because "Jesus thown everything off balance." The Misfit preaches the same radical Christian dualism from a different pulpit: "If He did what He said, then it's nothing for you to do but thow away everything and follow Him, and if He didn't, then it's nothing for you to do but enjoy the few minutes you got left the best way you can — by killing somebody or burning down his house or doing some other meanness to him. No pleasure but meanness." The Misfit has chosen the second alternative, but he admits at the end of the story, after wiping out the harmless family, "It's no real pleasure in life." Rufus lies and steals, he tells Sheppard, because "Satan . . . has me in his power," and in the course of the story he succeeds in converting Norton to Satanism (and thus to suicide), since, as Sheppard recognizes (in the story's central irony) but cannot understand, "The boy would rather be in hell than nowhere."

Another form God-intoxication paradoxically takes is Rationalism. The first of these antagonists in Miss O'Connor's work is the enigmatic figure of Mr. Paradise in "The River," who comes to the healings to mock and to display his unhealed cancerous ear, but who always comes. He is a curious ritual figure, the ceremonial scoffer, the Bishop of Misrule, and his shepherd's crook as mock-pastor is the giant peppermint stick with which he tries to save Harry from his death. Rayber is a fuller treatment of the same figure. He too is a mock-pastor (he named his son "Bishop"), and when old Tarwater baptized young Tarwater as a baby, Rayber then blasphemously baptized him a second time on the buttocks. Rayber has a catcher-in-the-rye "vision of himself moving like an avenging angel through the world, gathering up all the children that the Lord, not Herod, had slain," its Eden "some enclosed garden . . . where he would gather all the exploited children of the world and let the sunshine flood their minds." Rayber turns off the girl evangelist's indictment by turning off his hearing aid, but in his case we know, thanks to analyses by young Tarwater and by the author, that he is not deaf to Christianity but so responsive to it that all his positions are counter-positions. Rayber's views

35

caricature enlightened secular humanism by being stated as the negatives of Christian dogma, thus: "The great dignity of man," he tells young Tarwater, "is his ability to say: I am born once and no more."

If the male characters are all God-intoxicated, the female characters in Flannery O'Connor's fiction are mainly self-intoxicated. Smugness and self-satisfaction, often represented by women, is another important theme. Here is Mrs. Cope in "A Circle in the Fire" talking to Mrs. Pritchard: " 'Every day I say a prayer of thanksgiving,' Mrs. Cope said. 'Think of all we have. Lord,' she said and sighed, 'we have everything.' " The hoodlum boys who bring her to judgment state the truth she has forgotten: "Man, Gawd owns them woods and her too." Mrs. Cope, reciting all they have to be thankful for, "a litany of her blessings," becomes the monstrous comic figure of Mrs. Turpin in "Revelation." When she proclaims in the doctor's waiting room, "Thank you, Jesus, for making everything the way it is!" the Wellesley girl springs at her throat with a howl, throws a fit on the floor, and cries a revelation out of it, "Go back to hell where you came from, you old wart hog." This is a symbolic equivalent to the boys' judgment of Mrs. Cope, as the vision in which Mrs. Turpin sees the good Christians like herself in a hellfire in which "even their virtues were being burned away" is a symbolic equivalent to the boys' firing Mrs. Cope's woods.

In Flannery O'Connor's moral universe, in short, Hazel Motes may have backed himself into heaven, but fat Mrs. Turpin seems destined for hell. This dualism relates to another theme, the transvaluation of values in which progress in the world is retrogression in the spirit. When Mr. Shiftlet in "The Life You Save May Be Your Own" tells the old woman, "the monks of old slept in their coffins!" she replies, "They wasn't as advanced as we are." This is Miss O'Connor's standard joke. Old Tarwater speaks for the author when he tells the boy of Rayber's intention to give him "every advantage," and adds, "You have me to thank for saving you from those advantages."

It is thus necessary to imitate the monks of old, to deny the world, and Naysaying is another of Flannery O'Connor's major themes. "Flying is the greatest engineering achievement of man," Rayber says, and young Tarwater answers him, "I wouldn't give you nothing for no airplane. A buzzard can fly." Similarly, Mary Fortune denies that anyone has ever whipped her or ever could, although her grandfather has just seen her whipped; "I don't need no new shoe," Rufus Johnson insists to Sheppard, with his club-foot barely covered by the old torn shoe. These lying denials are a higher truth, the truth of the spirit that contradicts the weakness of the flesh.

Flannery O'Connor's meanings are not only Christian, they are Christian mainly in the mystic and ascetic tradition of St. John of the Cross ("Hence the soul cannot be possessed of the divine union, until it has divested itself of the love of created beings") rather than in the humanitarian tradition expressed in I John 4:20 ("If a man say, I love God, and hateth his brother, he is a liar").

Miss O'Connor is said to have been pleased when the London *Times* identified her as a "theological" writer. As a fiction-writing theologian, she seems the most radical Christian dualist since Dostoevski. There are two of everything in her work, one Christ's and one anti-Christ's. There are two wafers, and since Rayber rejects Christ's, "he felt the taste of his own childhood pain laid again on his tongue like a bitter wafer." There are two baptisms, the one old Tarwater gives and the one Rayber gives. There are two rivers in "The River," one "the rich red river of Jesus' Blood," the other the mundane river in which Mr. Paradise appears "like some ancient water monster." There are two fires in "A Circle in the Fire," one the fiery furnace in which the prophets dance, "in the circle the angel had cleared for them," the other set in the woods by the boys. The same two fires appear at the end of *The Violent*, when Tarwater raises himself from the ground, and "the burning bush had disappeared. A line of fire ate languidly at the treeline." There are two Hazes in *Wise Blood*, one a false prophet, and two young Tarwaters in *The Violent*, one of whom dissociates himself from the other as mad.

Miss O'Connor's subject is Vocation only in this radical dualist or tragic sense, that the way to sanctity is through the greatest sinfulness. She reported with pride to a friend that a young nun showed her full comprehension of *The Violent* when she said that she understood Tarwater perfectly: "He was struggling with his vocation. I've been through that — I know just how he felt and you did, too." The relationship between the two realms of experience, the young nun's spiritual struggle and Tarwater's criminal actions and passions, is analogical: murdering an idiot becomes a proper metaphor for Christian baptism, firing a woods a proper metaphor for Christian confirmation. In a time of desperate unbelief, in Miss O'Connor's view, the Christian sacraments must be understood to be equally desperate, and the language of desperation is violence and crime.

Two more thematic consequences of Flannery O'Connor's radical Christian dualism remain to be noticed. One is the False Christ. Hazel Motes says: "What do I need with Jesus? I got Leora Watts." When he leaves Mrs. Watts, the old Essex becomes his substitute Jesus. The car Mr. Shiftlet acquires by marrying and deserting the deaf girl is similarly a substitute Christ; when he finally gets it running "He had an expression of serious modesty on his face as if he had just raised the dead." Mr. Shiftlet explains his philosophy to the old woman: "The body, lady, is like a house: it don't go anywhere; but the spirit, lady, is like a automobile: always on the move." Thomas in "The Comforts of Home" and

Sheppard in "The Lame Shall Enter First" do not have false Christs, they *are* false Christs.

The remaining Christian theme is best put by St. Paul in I Corinthians 1:25, "Because the foolishness of God is wiser than men," and 3:19, "For the wisdom of this world is foolishness with God." The way to wisdom is through folly as the way to sanctity is through sin. Old Tarwater, taken to the insane asylum in a straitjacket for his wild prophesying, is God's Fool, and young Tarwater's vision of following "the bleeding stinking mad shadow of Jesus" hinges on the same paradox: Jesus' way is mad only by "the wisdom of this world."

Protestant Fundamentalism is thus Miss O'Connor's metaphor, in literary terms, for Roman Catholic truth (in theological terms, this reflects ecumenicism). Why did she see through a glass darkly, rather than face to face? There are many answers, and no certain answer. One answer that she gave to interviewers, that Protestant Fundamentalism was the milieu in which she grew up, is not really satisfactory. True, there are not many Catholics in rural Georgia, but then there are not many (or any) Hazes or Tarwaters either. Miss O'Connor gave a deeper answer in an interview with Granville Hicks: "I'm not interested in the sects as sects; I'm concerned with the religious individual, the backwoods prophet. Old Tarwater is the hero of *The Violent Bear It Away*, and I'm right behind him 100 per cent."

In a letter to Sister Mariella Gable O.S.B., quoted in the memorial issue of *Esprit*, she wrote: "People make a judgment of fanaticism by what they are themselves. To a lot of Protestants I know, monks and nuns are fanatics, none greater. And to a lot of monks and nuns I know, my Protestant prophets are fanatics. For my part, I think the only difference between them is that if you are a Catholic and have this intensity of belief you join the convent and are heard no more; whereas if you are a Protestant and have it, there

39

is no convent for you to join and you go about the world getting into all sorts of trouble and drawing the wrath of people who don't believe anything much at all down on your head. This is one reason why I can write about Protestant believers better than Catholic believers — because they express their belief in diverse kinds of dramatic action which is obvious enough for me to catch."

Whatever caused Miss O'Connor to choose Protestant Fundamentalism as her metaphor for Catholic vision, it was a brilliant choice. It gave her imagery that is naturally dramatistic, as she says, and, as she does not say, it freed her from the constraints of good taste — the young nun who identified her struggles with Tarwater's could not, as the protagonist of a novel, be made to undergo experiences comparable to his. The gains enormously outweigh the losses. If Flannery O'Connor, by choosing a tent revivalist subject matter, could not write such a portrait of serene saintliness as J. F. Powers' "Lions, Harts, and Leaping Does," in exchange she was spared the necessity of writing Powers' pious fables about the rectory cat. In any case, neither was in accord with her gifts or her temperament.

As a Catholic born and brought up in Georgia, Miss O'Connor always insisted, not only on her right to the imagery of southern Protestantism, but on its peculiar fitness for her as a Catholic. In a letter, she wrote: "Now the South is a good place for a Catholic literature in my sense for a number of reasons. 1) In the South belief can still be made believable and in relation to a large part of the society. We're not the Bible Belt for nothing. 2) The Bible being generally known and revered in the section, gives the novelist that broad mythical base to refer to that he needs to extend his meaning in depth. 3) The South has a sacramental view of life . . . 4) The aspect of Protestantism that is most prominent (at least to the Catholic) in the South is that of man dealing with God directly, not through the mediation of the church, and this is great for the Catholic novelist like myself who wants to get close to his character and watch him wrestle with the Lord."

Flannery O'Connor was a loyal Georgian and a loyal southerner, in her fashion. She was not only a southerner but a white southern lady. In one aspect this was an ironic stance. She told friends that she had not read *Lolita* because "White Southern ladies can't read such books," a remark she must often have heard about her own work. But it does not seem to have been an ironic stance in regard to the race question, on which Miss O'Connor maintained a consistent public silence. There are, however, curious symbolic statements in her work. "Her fiction does not reflect the social issues, particularly the racial problems, which beset the South during her lifetime," says John J. Clarke in *Esprit*. I think that it does, and more powerfully and truly than that of anyone else, but the expression is always implicit, covert, cryptic. As her mad prophets are metaphoric for Roman Catholic truth, so in a sense all the fierce violence in her work is metaphoric for violence done the Negro. This is most clear in *Wise Blood*, when ten-year-old Haze is trying to figure out what dirty mystery is going on in the carnival tent. We follow the sequence of his thoughts from "It's some men in a privy," to "maybe it's a man and a woman in a privy," to his sudden question to the barker: "Is it a nigger? . . . Are they doing something to a nigger?" (I would exchange many high-minded tracts on the Question for the insight in that progression.)

The Negroes in the stories are seen externally, as a conventional white southern lady would see them, with no access to their concealed sensibility, but occasionally one of them will say something (there are several such remarks in "The Displaced Person") that shows how much the author knows about that sensibility. Negroes in the fiction sometimes carry profound spiritual meaning, as in "The Artificial Nigger" or in the figure of Buford Munson in *The*

Violent. In several stories, and in the fragment of the unfinished novel, Negroes are images of fraternity. In the deepest sense, Harry in "The River," who goes to his death because he wants to *count*, or Norton in "The Lame Shall Enter First," who hangs himself because he wants to be *some*where, are symbols for Negro aspirations and frustrations; they are symbolic Negroes or "artificial niggers," in fact, and the author knew it.

Which brings us to the question of integration. Mr. Guizac, the displaced person, is a full integrationist out of desperation: he is trying to marry his sixteen-year-old Polish cousin to the Negro Sulk, to get her out of the refugee camps. It is this project, which Mrs. McIntyre characteristically describes as a match between a "poor innocent child" and a "half-witted thieving black stinking nigger," that leads to his fall from Mrs. McIntyre's favor and thus to his fate. Mr. Guizac's integrationist slogan is minimal: "She no care black. . . . She in camp three year." Insofar as he embodies Christ the Displaced Person, however, his implicit integrationist slogan is maximal: God died to redeem all mankind.

Integrationism is savagely travestied as sentimental and fatuous in Julian in "Everything That Rises Must Converge" and Asbury in "The Enduring Chill," but the opposing view is just as savagely travestied in their mothers. "They should rise, yes, but on their own side of the fence," Julian's mother says, and the title, as well as her stroke, is the rejoinder.

We understand the nature of Miss O'Connor's opposition to integration when we see Asbury think of smoking with the Negroes who work for his mother as "one of those moments of communion when the difference between black and white is absorbed into nothing." In Miss O'Connor's radical Christian dualism, this is a secular and thus a false communion, and integration in general is a secular and thus a false salvation. Whereas her friend Father Merton finds integration so deeply inherent in the Christian concept of Incarnation that he regards any trace of racism in a Roman Catholic as automatically self-excommunicating, Miss O'Connor insists with Dostoevski that the only equality is to be found in the spiritual dignity of man, in the mystic communion of the Sacraments.

It is not easy to place Flannery O'Connor in a literary tradition. The writer to whom she is most indebted stylistically, Mark Twain, is never mentioned in discussions of her work, nor did she ever identify him as an influence, so far as I know. Yet if *The Violent Bear It Away* has any single progenitor, it is *Adventures of Huckleberry Finn*. Miss O'Connor's mature writing has very little to do with Faulkner or any of what is called "southern" literature. The writer who most influenced her, at least in her first books, is Nathanael West. *Wise Blood* is clearly modeled on *Miss Lonelyhearts* (as no reviewer noticed at the time), and contains many specific reminiscences of it. Hazel Motes has a nose "like a shrike's bill"; after he goes to bed with Leora Watts, Haze feels "like something washed ashore on her"; Sabbath Lily's correspondence with a newspaper advice-columnist is purest West; and all the rocks in *Wise Blood* recall the rock Miss Lonelyhearts first contains in his gut and then becomes, the rock on which the new Peter will found the new Church. The European writer Flannery O'Connor most profoundly resembles (in method, not in scale) is Dostoevski. Like him she created a deeply understood Enemy out of her own liberal and enlightened dreams. "Ivan Karamazov cannot believe," she wrote in her introduction to *A Memoir of Mary Ann*, "as long as one child is in torment" — no more can Rayber or Sheppard, she might have added.

It is surely too early to evaluate Flannery O'Connor's work or place it in our literature, but some beginnings can be attempted. Two points must be made immediately. The first is that despite the prevailing opinion, she was primarily a novelist, not a short story writer, and consequently her novels are better and more important than even the best of her stories. The second is that any discussion of her theology can only be preliminary to, not a substitute for, aesthetic analysis and evaluation.

The strengths of Flannery O'Connor's writing are those qualities in it that have been most disliked and attacked: the apocalyptic violence, the grotesque vision, the vulgarity. "Her novels suffer, I believe, from an excessive violence of conception," Warren Coffey wrote in *Esprit*, contrasting them with her stories. But it is precisely this violence in the novels — these murders and burnings, blindings and rapes — that is the heart of their imaginative power, as is murder in Dostoevski's novels. It is the violence of desperate Christianity, of the desperate and verbally inarticulate South, of a nation no longer quiet about its desperation. William Esty wrote scornfully, in *Commonweal*, of Flannery O'Connor's "cult of the Gratuitous Grotesque." Her fiction is grotesque, certainly, but never gratuitously so. For example, in the opening scene of "The Lame Shall Enter First," Norton eats a piece of chocolate cake spread with peanut butter and ketchup; when his father gets him upset, he vomits it all up in "a limp sweet batter." This is not only grotesque but thoroughly repulsive, and no less repulsive to the author, but it is entirely functional and necessary in the story: it perfectly symbolizes the indigestible mess of Sheppard's "enlightened" views, which Norton will similarly be unable to keep down. Flannery O'Connor herself answered the charge definitively in an unpublished lecture: "I have found that any fiction that comes out of the South is going to be considered grotesque by the Northern critic, unless it is grotesque, in which case it is going to be considered realistic." Nor is this merely a matter of the northern critic. All art, to the extent that it is new and serious, is shocking and disturbing, and one way of dismissing those truths that get through to us is as "grotesque."

We must not ignore the weaknesses of Flannery O'Connor's fiction. Her stories came to rely too often and too mechanically on death to end them. The deaths are ruinous to "A View of the Woods," and unnecessary in other stories. Her best stories — "The Artificial Nigger," "Good Country People," "Parker's Back" — neither end in death nor need to. One reason for her melodramatic endings seems to be theological. "I'm a born Catholic and death has always been brother to my imagination," Miss O'Connor told an interviewer in *Jubilee*, "I can't imagine a story that doesn't properly end in it or in its foreshadowings." It was one of her rare confusions of theology with aesthetics.

These endings result from a misjudgment in craft, as do those occasions — in "Good Country People" and "A View of the Woods" — in which she runs on past a story's natural finish. Other than these, the only fault in her fiction is a tendency to travesty. Caricature is a legitimate resource of art, and a magnificently effective one in her hands, but her caricature sometimes fell into over-caricature and lost its truth, so that we cannot believe in the existence of certain of her secular intellectuals or Negroes. If they are not people, they cannot function as symbols, since, as she says in the lecture on the grotesque, "It is the nature of fiction not to be good for much else unless it is good in itself."

Flannery O'Connor's fiction is a powerful example of what Kenneth Burke calls "symbolic action," functioning for the author as well as for the reader. The root meaning of "caricature" is "overload," and in this sense Miss O'Connor created characters and their dramatic oppositions by separating, exaggerating, and polarizing elements in herself. The Tarwaters and Rayber are the Yang and Yin of the author, each made extreme, in just the fashion that Stephen and Bloom are, or Ahab and Ishmael. These opposites held in tension externalize an inner war, but they do so dramatically and they progress to a dramatic resolution, in the process exorcising ambivalence and resolving doubt. "I have written a wicked book," Melville wrote to Hawthorne when he had finished *Moby-Dick*, "and feel spotless as the lamb." As Dostoevski could find all that was most detestable, Stavrogin and Smerdyakov, deep inside himself, so Miss O'Connor could find inside herself Hazel Motes, the blind fanatic, and Joy-Hulga, the spiteful atheist. And in finding them, in incarnating them in art, she rid herself of them. The stories are full of bitter hate *in order that* the author may be friendly and loving; the novels scream doubt and denial *in order that* the author may be devout and serene.

As this symbolic action transforms the author, so it transforms the reader. We undergo these terrible events, as horror-filled as Greek tragedy, to be purged and sweetened, even kept devout (in our different devotions). Few of Flannery O'Connor's readers, few even of her Roman Catholic readers, can share her desperate and radical Christian dualism, as she was fully aware. But it constituted a natural dramatism for fiction, as did Dostoevski's religion, and a fiction in no sense parochial. As a writer she had the additional advantage, as West did, of multiple alienation from the dominant assumptions of our culture: he was an outsider as a Jew, and doubly an outsider as a Jew alienated from other Jews; she was comparably an outsider as a woman, a southerner, and a Roman Catholic in the South. This is not to say that her views, or her alienation, produced the fiction; many have held more radical views, and been far more alienated, while producing nothing. Her gifts produced the fiction, but her situation gave them opportunities, and enabled her to exercise her intelligence, imagination, and craft most effectively. Her early death may have deprived the world of unforeseeable marvels, but she left us, in *The Violent Bear It Away*, parts of *Wise Blood*, and the best stories, marvels enough.

⊀ Selected Bibliography

Works of Flannery O'Connor

Wise Blood. New York: Harcourt, Brace, 1952.
A Good Man Is Hard to Find. New York: Harcourt, Brace, 1955.
The Violent Bear It Away. New York: Farrar, Straus, and Cudahy, 1960.
Everything That Rises Must Converge. New York: Farrar, Straus, and Giroux, 1965. (With an introduction by Robert Fitzgerald.)
"The Fiction Writer and His Country," in *The Living Novel,* edited by Granville Hicks. New York: Macmillan, 1957. Pp. 157–64.
"The Church and the Fiction Writer," *America,* 96:733–35 (March 30, 1957).
"Living with a Peacock," *Holiday,* 30:52 (September 1961).
Introduction to *A Memoir of Mary Ann.* New York: Farrar, Straus, and Cudahy, 1961, 1962.
Note on *The Phenomenon of Man,* by Pierre Teilhard de Chardin, *American Scholar,* 30:618 (Fall 1961).
"The Regional Writer," *Esprit,* 7:31–35 (Winter 1963).
"Why Do the Heathens Rage?" *Esquire,* 60:60–61 (July 1963).
"The Role of the Catholic Novelist," *Greyfriar,* 7:5–12 (1964).

Current American Reprint

Three by Flannery O'Connor. New York: Signet. $.95.

Critical and Biographical Studies

Baumbach, Jonathan. "The Acid of God's Grace: *Wise Blood* by Flannery O'Connor," in *The Landscape of Nightmare.* New York: New York University Press, 1965. Pp. 87–100.
Critique, Vol. 2, No. 2 (Fall 1958). (An issue jointly devoted to Flannery O'Connor and J. F. Powers, with a bibliography and articles on the former by Caroline Gordon, Sister M. Bernetta Quinn O.S.F., Louis D. Rubin, Jr., and George F. Wedge.)
Esprit, Vol. 8, No. 1 (Winter 1964). (A memorial issue.)
Farnham, James F. "The Grotesque in Flannery O'Connor," *America,* 105:277–81 (May 13, 1961).
Ferris, Sumner J. "The Outside and the Inside: Flannery O'Connor's *The Violent Bear It Away,*" *Critique,* 3:11–19 (Winter–Spring 1960).

Fitzgerald, Robert. "The Countryside and the True Country," *Sewanee Review*, 70:380–94 (Summer 1962).

Friedman, M. J. "Flannery O'Connor: Another Legend in Southern Fiction," in Joseph J. Waldmeir, ed., *Recent American Fiction: Some Critical Views*. Boston: Houghton Mifflin, 1963. Pp. 231–45.

Gable, Sister Mariella, O.S.B. "Ecumenic Core in Flannery O'Connor's Fiction," *American Benedictine Review*, 15:127–43 (June 1964).

Gossett, Louise Y. "The Test by Fire: Flannery O'Connor," *Violence in Recent Southern Fiction*. Durham, N.C.: Duke University Press, 1965. Pp. 75–97.

Hart, Jane. "Strange Earth: The Stories of Flannery O'Connor," *Georgia Review*, 12:215–22 (Summer 1958).

Hawkes, John. "Flannery O'Connor's Devil," *Sewanee Review*, 70:395–407 (Summer 1962).

Hicks, Granville. "A Writer at Home with Her Heritage," *Saturday Review*, 45:22–23 (May 12, 1962).

––––––. "A Cold, Hard Look at Humankind," *Saturday Review*, 48:23–24 (May 29, 1965).

Hyman, Stanley Edgar. "Flannery O'Connor's Tattooed Christ," *New Leader*, 48:9–10 (May 10, 1965).

Joselyn, Sister M., O.S.B. "Thematic Centers in 'The Displaced Person,'" *Studies in Short Fiction*, 1:85–92 (Winter 1964).

Malin, Irving. *New American Gothic*. Carbondale: Southern Illinois University Press, 1962. *Passim*.

Meaders, Margaret Inman. "Flannery O'Connor: 'Literary Witch,'" *Colorado Quarterly*, 10:377–86 (Spring 1962).

[Meyers], Sister Bertrande, D.C. "Four Stories of Flannery O'Connor," *Thought*, 37:410–26 (Autumn 1962).

Rose Alice, Sister, S.S.J. "Flannery O'Connor: Poet to the Outcast," *Renascence*, 16:126–32 (Spring 1964).

Solotaroff, Theodore. "You *Can* Go Home Again," *Book Week*, 2:1, 13 (May 30, 1965).

Spivey, Ted R. "Flannery O'Connor's View of God and Man," *Studies in Short Fiction*, 1:200–6 (Spring 1964).

Stelzmann, Rainulf A. "Shock and Orthodoxy: An Interpretation of Flannery O'Connor's Novels and Short Stories," *Xavier University Studies*, 2:1 (March 1963).

Stern, Richard. "Flannery O'Connor: A Remembrance and Some Letters," *Shenandoah*, 16:5–10 (Winter 1965).

Tate, Mary Barbara. "Flannery O'Connor: A Reminiscence," *Columns*, 2:1 (Fall 1964).

3H01274

PS   Hyman, Stanley Edgar
3565   Flannery O'Connor
C5.7
Z7

Normandale State Junior College

9700 France Avenue South

Bloomington, Minnesota 55437

DEMCO